# ROOTS and ROUTES

## A Dictionary of Word Derivations

Sylvia Karavis and Catherine Byrne

For Paul – S.K.

Heinemann is an imprint of Pearson Education
Limited, a company incorporated in England
and Wales, having its registered office at
Edinburgh Gate, Harlow, Essex, CM20 2JE.
Registered company number: 872828

Heinemann is a registered trademark of Pearson Education Limited

OXFORD MELBOURNE AUCKLAND
JOHANNESBURG BLANTYRE GABORONE
IBADAN PORTSMOUTH (NH) USA CHICAGO



First published 1999

10 09
10 9 8 7

British Library Cataloguing in Publication Data
A catalogue record for this book is available from the British Library.

ISBN 978 0 435 09693 9 *Roots and Routes* single copy

ISBN 978 0 435 09694 6 *Roots and Routes* 6 copy pack



All illustrations by Phil Healey.

Printed and bound in China (CTPS/07)

# Contents

# Introduction

Languages grow and change over time, adapting to the needs of the people using them. English is no exception. New words are constantly being added and others die out. English is spoken in Great Britain, the United States, Australia, New Zealand and Canada, and is the first language of millions of people. It is the official language of the United Nations, international air-traffic control and shipping and is used widely in international business, computing and science.

## History

> It is believed that all European languages originated from one language: Indo-European. It is thought that many thousands of years ago, this language was spoken by the nomadic tribes that inhabited Eastern Europe. As the tribes spread, travelled west and settled, different languages developed.

The earliest inhabitants of Britain would have spoken Celtic, from which present-day Welsh, Gaelic and Irish developed. The first big influences on the spoken language came when Britain was invaded between 450 and 700 AD by the Angles, Saxons and Jutes, who came from Northern Europe. These people introduced their own languages into Britain and drove the speakers of Celtic north and west. Gradually, Anglo-Saxon became the main language of Britain. Much of the English spoken today can be traced back to Anglo-Saxon times. For example, language that describes everyday activities such as the words for *home*, *eat*, *sleep* and *food* originated from this time. In dictionaries, words originating from Anglo-Saxon are referred to as Old English (OE).

The next invasion came between 740 and 1050 AD, from the Vikings, who also introduced many new words into English. The Vikings came from Norway and Denmark and spoke a language we now call Old Norse.

The Normans invaded Britain in 1066. These people, from northern France, brought about great changes to the way in which people lived and the language they used. French became the language of authority, and many new words connected to law, government and power were introduced. Ordinary people continued to speak English, but gradually many words were introduced into the everyday language. The language spoken at this time, a mixture of Old English and Norman French, is known as Middle English (ME).

During the 6th century, other influences on the English language came from missionaries, who not only wrote in Latin, but also began to write down Anglo-Saxon using the Latin alphabet. This became the earliest English alphabet. Around this period, other scholarly languages such as Hebrew and Greek also influenced English. However, of these, Latin has probably had the greatest impact.

The Renaissance, literally the 'rebirth' of interest in Greek and Roman art and learning, began in Italy in the 15th century, and spread to other parts of Europe during the 16th century. This movement introduced many Italian words connected to the arts, technology and engineering into the languages of northern Europe.

English was influenced not only by people coming into Britain, but also by travellers returning from exploration and trading expeditions. From about 1500 Britain became a nation of trade and colonisation. English was introduced into other parts of the world and, inevitably, travellers returning to Britain brought words from other languages back with them. This continues to happen today.

During the 20th century, many people from other countries settled in Britain, introducing elements of other cultures and languages. This process continues to expand and enrich the English we use today. Sometimes there is no concise equivalent for a particular phrase, usually because the adaptation would be too lengthy. In these cases, the word or phrase is adopted in its original form and becomes part of everyday English. (See Appendix 1: Loan words.)

Language describes and names who we are, what we do and use, where we live and how we behave. New events, inventions and situations require new words. Often these words already exist but begin to be used in new contexts. They acquire slightly different or alternative meanings, and sometimes altered spellings. The 20th century in particular has seen the introduction of a huge new technological vocabulary, e.g. *byte*, *cursor*, *disk*. However, the words in this dictionary have been selected because of their everyday relevance and their interesting origins, and are, for the most part, pre-20th century.

The following linguistic terms are used in this dictionary:

**acronym** a word formed from the first letter or letters of several words, e.g. RSPCA from **R**oyal **S**ociety for the **P**revention of **C**ruelty to **A**nimals.

**anagram** a word made by rearranging the letters of another word, e.g. *march* is an anagram of *charm*.

**back slang** slang in which words are spoken as if they were spelled backwards, e.g. *redraw* for *warder*.

**dialect** the version of a language spoken in a particular part of the country or by a particular group of people.

**imitative** a word that copies a natural sound, e.g. *fizz*.

**slang** everyday, casual language consisting of words used in an informal way.

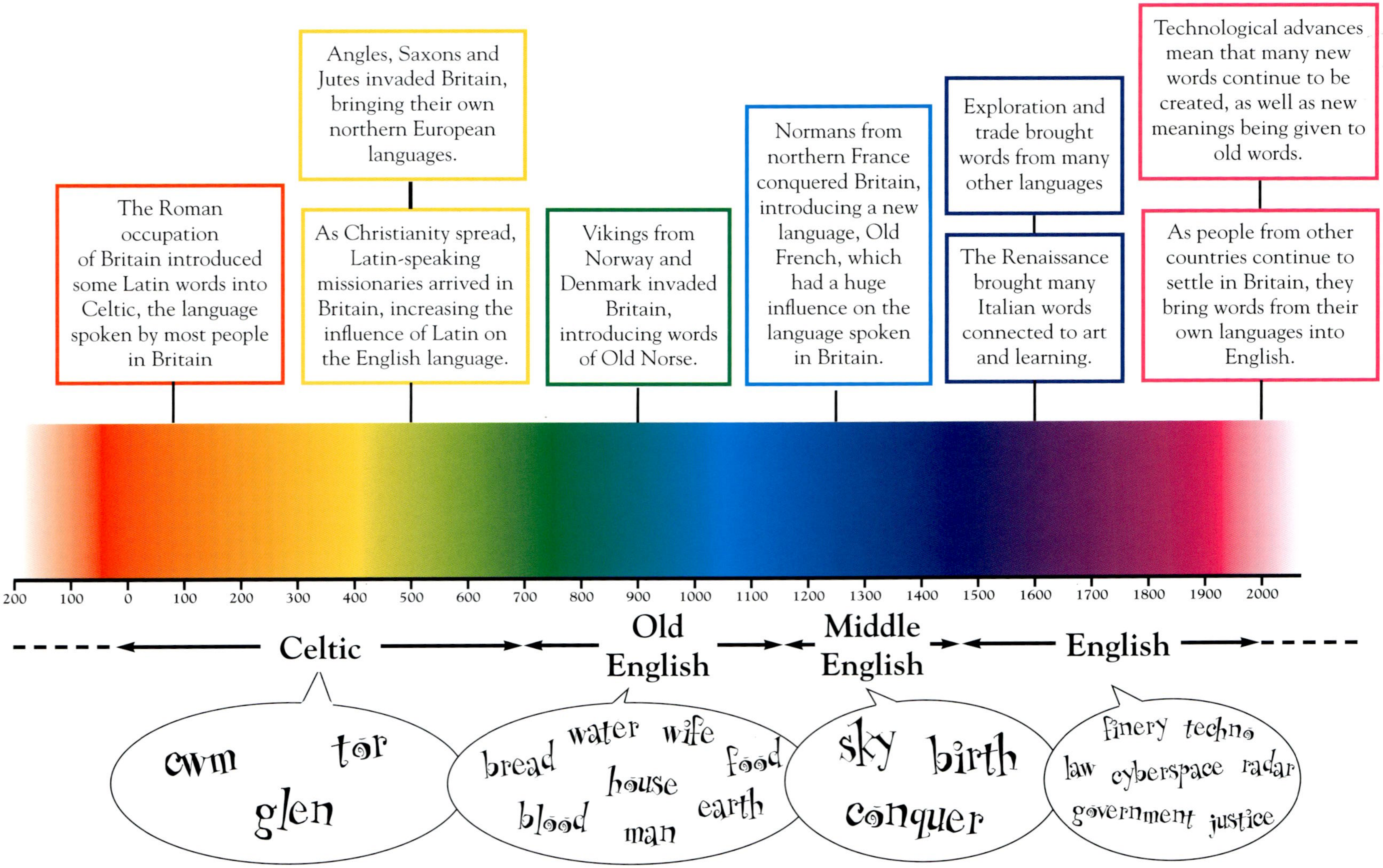


This timeline shows the major influences on the development of the English language.

# Language map

This language map shows how Indo-European spread and developed into different languages.

# How this dictionary works

The headword is in **bold**.

If the word is used informally (slang), this information is given immediately after the headword.

**bloke** informal
***noun*** man.
**origin** C19, from Shelta *bloke* 'man'. Shelta was an ancient secret language, based on Irish and Gaelic, used by Irish and Welsh gypsies.

The word's meaning or meanings.

The part of speech is in ***bold italics***.

The original form of the word in italics followed by the English translation in inverted commas.

The entry may give further information on the route between the origin and the current meaning.

The period, century or date that the word was introduced into English.

The language from which the word came, if known (in some cases it is uncertain how a word originated).

Many words change their function according to context, and therefore their grammatical description also changes. In this dictionary, the part of speech, or grammatical description, given is the sense in which the word is most commonly used, e.g. *barbecue* – noun; *escape* – verb.

Cross-references are in SMALL CAPITALS, e.g. 'see UMBRELLA'.

Sometimes more than one meaning is given for a word, because the word has different strands of meaning, e.g. *magazine*, *tank*.

**abacus**
***noun*** a rectangular frame with rows of beads on wires, used for counting.
**origin** ME, from Latin, from Greek *abax, abak* 'board strewn with sand on which to draw or make marks', probably from Hebrew *āḇāq* 'dust'.

**adder**
***noun*** small venomous snake with dark zigzag on its back, the only poisonous snake in Britain, also known as a 'viper'.
**origin** OE *naedre* 'serpent'. The *n* was lost by wrong division of *a naddre*.

**aftermath**
***noun*** the effects or consequences of an event, usually unpleasant.
**origin** C15 *aftermath* 'second crop of grass after the first mowing', from 'after' + the dialect word *math* 'mowing'.

**alcohol**
***noun*** an intoxicating liquid present in beer, wine and spirits.
**origin** C16, from Arabic *al-kuḥl* 'the kohl'. Kohl is a fine powder used as a cosmetic to stain the skin. The current meaning dates from C17.

**alligator**
***noun*** a large semi-aquatic reptile, similar to a crocodile but with a shorter, broader head.
**origin** C16, from Spanish *el lagarto* 'the lizard'.

**anthology**
***noun*** collection of writings by different authors.
**origin** C17, from Greek *anthos* 'flower' + *logia* 'collection'. The word originally meant a collection of 'the flowers of verse'.

**apartheid**
***noun*** the policy of segregation on the grounds of race.
**origin** 1940s, from Afrikaans, literally 'separateness'.

**apron**
***noun*** a protective garment worn over clothes and tied at the back.
**origin** ME *naperon*, from French *nape, nappe* 'tablecloth'. The *n* was lost by wrong division of *a napron*.

**arena**
***noun*** a level area surrounded by seating where sports and entertainments are held.
**origin** C17, from Latin *harena* 'sand', *arena* 'sand-strewn place of combat'.

**atlas**
***noun*** a book of maps or charts.
**origin** C16, from Greek *Atlas*. According to Greek mythology, Atlas the Titan was punished by the gods and made to hold up the heavens. The Atlas mountains in North Africa were named after him, and his figure often appeared on the front of books of maps, which became known as atlases.

**attitude**
***noun*** a way of thinking or behaving, sometimes reflected in behaviour.
**origin** C17, from Latin *aptus* 'fit'. 'Attitude' was originally a fine-art term meaning the position of a figure in sculpture or painting.

**badger**
***noun*** a nocturnal mammal with a distinctive black and grey coat.
**origin** C16, perhaps from 'badge', because of the pale markings on its head.

**balaclava**
***noun*** close-fitting hood covering the whole head and neck with an opening for the face.
**origin** C19, short for *Balaclava helmet*, a hood worn by soldiers during the Crimean War, named after the village of Balaclava in the Crimea.

**bald**
***adjective*** having no hair.
**origin** ME, meaning 'white patch'. A bald eagle is an eagle with white feathers on its face and neck.

**ballot**
***noun*** a method of voting on a specified issue.
**origin** C16, from Italian *ballotta* 'small ball'. Once, a coloured ball was placed in a container to register a vote.

**bandanna**
***noun*** scarf or handkerchief, usually of one colour with white spots.
**origin** C18, probably from Hindi *bandhnu* 'tie-dye' or Portuguese *bandana*.

**bankrupt**
***adjective*** declared by law to be unable to pay financial debts.
**origin** C16, from Italian *banca rotta* 'broken bench'. Banking and money-lending was conducted on benches in an open-air market. When someone could no longer carry on business through owing more money than they had, their bench would have been dismantled.

**barbecue**
***noun*** a meal or gathering where food is cooked in the open on a rack over a fire.
**origin** C17, from Spanish *barbacoa*, perhaps from Haitian *barbacoa* 'wooden frame on posts for sleeping on or for storing meat or fish to be dried'. Today, the word 'barbecue' also refers to the rack or the appliance on which the food is cooked.

**belladonna**
***noun*** another word for the plant 'deadly nightshade'.
**origin** C18, from Italian *bella donna* 'fair lady', perhaps because the juice was used to add brilliance to the eyes.

**biscuit**
***noun*** a flat, thin cake, baked to be dry and crisp.
**origin** ME, from French *bescuit*, from Latin *bis* 'twice' + *coquere* 'to cook'. Biscuits were originally cooked twice – once baked, and then dried out in a slow oven so that they would keep.

**bloke** informal
***noun*** man.
**origin** C19, from Shelta *bloke* 'man'. Shelta was an ancient secret language, based on Irish and Gaelic, used by Irish and Welsh gypsies.

**bogus**
***adjective*** fake.
**origin** C18. The word was originally used in US English, and meant 'machine for making counterfeit money'.

**brash**
***adjective*** noisy, tasteless, over-bright.
**origin** C19, originally a dialect word, possibly from *rash* 'acting without consideration of consequences'.

**bungalow**
***noun*** a single-storied house.
**origin** C17, from Gujarati *bangalo*, Hindi *baṅglā* 'belonging to Bengal'. There were many single-storied houses in Bengal.

**buzz**
***noun*** sound such as that made by a bee or other insect.
**origin** ME, imitative.

**cagoule**
***noun*** a very light, hooded, waterproof jacket worn over other clothes.
**origin** 1950s, from French, literally 'cowl' or 'hood'.

**calculate**
***verb*** to find out by means of mathematics.
**origin** ME, from Latin *calculus* 'pebble, such as those used in an abacus'. See ABACUS.

**caravan**
***noun*** a vehicle for living in, usually towed.
**origin** C15, from French *caravane*, from Persian *kārwān* 'group of travellers banded together for safety'. The current sense dates from C19.

**carnival**
***noun*** public festival, usually with a procession, music and dancing.
**origin** C16, from Italian *carnevale*, from Latin *carnelevarium* 'Shrovetide', from Latin *carne* 'meat' + *levare* 'to put away'. Shrovetide was the name for the celebrations before people gave up eating meat for Lent.

**catamaran**
***noun*** a boat with two hulls.
**origin** C17, from Tamil *kattumaram* 'tied wood'.

**chocolate**
**noun** a confection, usually in a slab, made from cacao powder and sugar.
**origin** C17, from Nahuatl *chocolatl* 'food made from cacao seeds', via Spanish and French. Chocolate was originally a drink. In 1664 Samuel Pepys wrote about drinking 'jocolatte'.

**chrysanthemum**
***noun*** brightly coloured, daisy-like flower.
**origin** from Greek *khrusos* 'gold' + *anthemon* 'flower'.

**cliché**
***noun*** phrase or opinion that is overused and demonstrates a lack of originality.
**origin** C19, from French *clicher* 'to stereotype'. A stereotype plate in printing is one cast from an original plate.

**coach**
***noun*** single-decker bus used for long journeys.
**origin** C16, from Hungarian *kocsi szekér* 'wagon from Kocs'. Kocs is a town in Hungary where the first large four-wheeled vehicle was invented.

**confetti**
***noun*** small pieces of coloured paper traditionally thrown over the bride and groom at a wedding.
**origin** C19, from Italian *confetto* 'sweet'. Sweets were thrown during carnivals. See CARNIVAL.

**conker**
***noun*** the hard, shiny, brown nut of the horse chestnut tree.
**origin** C19, originally a dialect word for a snail shell, with which the game of conkers used to be played, probably from Greek *konkhe* 'shell'. In C19 and C20, the game of conkers was sometimes called 'conquerers'.

**corduroy**
***noun*** thick cotton fabric, ribbed and velvety on one side.
**origin** C18, probably from *cord* 'ribbed fabric' + *duroy*, a kind of woollen cloth made in the West of England.

**corridor**
***noun*** a long passage in a building, usually with doors opening into rooms.
**origin** C16, from Latin *currere* 'to run'. The word was originally a military term for a strip of land on the edge of a ditch, protected by a parapet. The current meaning dates from C19.

**cot**
***noun*** bed with high sides for a baby.
**origin** C17, from Hindi *khāt* 'bedstead or hammock'. The US use of 'cot' to mean 'campbed' is nearer the original meaning.

**cotton**
***noun*** material or thread made from soft white fibres of the cotton plant.
**origin** C14, from French *coton*, from Arabic *ḳuṭn*.

**crash**
***noun*** violent collision.
**origin** ME, imitative. Perhaps a combination of 'craze' and 'dash'.

**crocodile**
***noun*** large semi-aquatic reptile with long jaws and tail, short legs and rough skin.
**origin** ME, from Greek *krokodilos* 'worm of the stones', from *kroke* 'pebble' + *drilos* 'worm'.

## cursor
*noun* the marker on a visual display screen, which moves to show where the next character or letter will appear.
**origin** ME, literally 'running messenger', from Latin *curs* 'run'.

## curtail
*verb* to stop, to cut short.
**origin** C16 *curtal* 'horse with a docked tail', from French *court* 'short', from Latin *curtus* 'short'.

## daisy
*noun* small flower with yellow centre and white petals.
**origin** OE *daeges eage* 'day's eye', because the flower opens in the morning and closes at night.

## dandelion
*noun* a common weed with yellow flowers and jagged leaves.
**origin** ME, from French *dent-de-lion* 'lion's tooth', from Latin *dens leonis* 'lion's tooth'. The plant was given this name because of the jagged shape of its leaves.

## danger
*noun* possibility of suffering harm.
**origin** ME, from French *dangier*, from Latin *dominus* 'lord'. The word originally meant 'power', or 'power to cause harm'.

## deck
*noun* the floor of a ship, especially the upper, open level.
*verb* to cover or clothe.
**origin** C15, from Dutch *dec* 'roof' or 'cloak', from Dutch *dekken* 'to cover'. The word once meant the canvas cover used on ships. Later it was used to mean the solid surface which served as a roof or floor.

## deer
*noun* hoofed, four-legged animal, the male having bony antlers.
**origin** OE *deor,* a word for any small four-legged wild animal' from Dutch *dier*.

## denim
*noun* coarse cotton fabric.
**origin** C17, short for *serge de Nimes*, a woollen fabric from Nimes, a town in the South of France.

## dinghy
*noun* small rowing boat.
**origin** C19, from Hindi *dingi*, *dengi* 'rowing boat used on Indian rivers'.

## dismal
*adjective* depressing, dreary
**origin** ME, from old French *dis mal* 'bad days', referring to the two days in every month that in medieval times were considered to be unlucky, from Latin *dies mali* 'evil days'.

## dungarees
*noun* pair of overalls, pair of trousers with a bib.
**origin** C17, from Hindi *duṅgrī* 'coarse calico fabric'.

## eavesdrop
*verb* to listen secretly to other people's conversation.
**origin** C17, from Old Norse *upsardropi*, from *ups* 'eaves' + *dropi* 'drop of water'. 'Eavesdrop' literally means 'the place where the water drips from the eaves'. An 'eavesdropper' is a person who listens from under the eaves to conversations taking place inside the house.

## electricity
*noun* form of energy resulting from charged particles.
**origin** C17, from Greek *electrum* 'amber'. An electrical charge can be created by rubbing amber.

**engine**
***noun*** machine that uses energy to create movement.
**origin** ME, from Latin *ingenium* 'talent', device'. The original meaning of 'engine' was something, such as a tool or weapon, created using ingenuity or cunning. The current meaning dates from C17.

**escape**
***verb*** to break free.
**origin** ME, from French *eschaper*, from Latin *ex* 'out' + *cappa* 'cloak'.

**explode**
***verb*** to burst violently into tiny pieces.
**origin** C16, from Latin *explodere* 'to drive out by clapping', 'to hiss off the stage', from *ex* 'out' + *plaudere* 'to clap'. The current meaning dates from C18.

**fan**
***noun*** someone who is devoted to a particular person, idea or activity.
**origin** C19. The word was originally used in US English as an abbreviation of 'fanatic'.

**flour**
***noun*** powder made from ground grain, used in cooking.
**origin** ME, possibly from French *fleur de farine* 'flower of wheat' or from 'flower', meaning 'the best part' of the grain. The spelling 'flower' for 'flour' was often used until C19.

**focus**
***noun*** the centre, the main point of an activity.
**origin** C17, from Latin, literally 'fireplace'. The fireplace can be considered the central point in a room. 'Focus' also came to mean the way in which fire can be created by focusing the sun's rays through a lens.

**fuchsia**
***noun*** shrub with hanging flowers, often in two contrasting colours.
**origin** C16, from the name of the botanist Leonhard Fuchs who brought it to Europe.

**gargoyle**
***noun*** ugly, distorted human or animal face made of stone, usually at the end of a gutter, acting as a rain-water spout.
**origin** ME, from French *gargouille* 'throat', probably from Greek *gargarizein* 'to gargle', an imitative word to describe the noise made from the throat.

**gas**
***noun*** air-like substance.
**origin** C17, from Greek *khaos* 'vast chasm', 'void', first coined by Belgian chemist J. B. van Helmont to describe the intangible or supernatural quality he believed existed in all matter.

**gimmick**
***noun*** something used to attract attention or publicity, often in advertising.
**origin** 1920s. The word was originally used in US English. It may derive from an anagram of 'magic', as the word originally meant 'a magician's apparatus'.

**glasnost**
***noun*** openness.
**origin** 1985, from Russian, literally 'the fact of being public'. The word was used to describe the policy of the former USSR to be more open, particularly in reporting news.

**gossip**
***noun*** conversation, particularly concerning other people, not necessarily based on truth.
**origin** OE *godsibb* 'godfather, godmother, godchild', from *god* 'God' + *sibb* 'relation'. In ME the word came to mean 'a close friend'. The current meaning dates from C19.

**happy**
***adjective*** feeling contentment or pleasure.
**origin** ME, from *hap* 'luck', 'chance', 'destiny'. 'Happy' originally meant 'lucky'.

**hell**
***noun*** in many religions a place of evil and suffering.
**origin** OE *hel*, *hell*, from Dutch *hel* 'covered, hidden place'. 'Helmet' also comes from the same root.

## huff
***verb*** to blow out noisily, to puff.
**origin** C16, imitative of sound of blowing.

## hum
***noun*** continuous sound.
**origin** ME, imitative.

## hurricane
***noun*** a storm with a strong wind, often in the Caribbean.
**origin** C16, from Spanish *huracan*, probably from Taino *hurakan* 'god of the storm'. Taino is an extinct language from the Caribbean.

## husband
***noun*** married man, male counterpart of 'wife'.
**origin** OE, meaning 'male head of household' or 'manager', not necessarily married. From Norse *hus* 'house' + *bondi* 'occupier', 'tiller of the soil'. The original sense of the word was 'farmer'. The word *wife* comes from OE *wif* 'woman'.

## illustration
***noun*** graphic representation, picture, drawing, photograph, diagram.
**origin** ME, from Latin *illustratio* 'illumination', 'spiritual or intellectual enlightenment'. The verb 'illustrate' came into current use in C16, literally meaning 'to throw light upon'.

## infantry
***noun*** foot soldiers.
**origin** C16, from Latin *infant* 'unable to speak'. Infantry were boys who were too young to serve in the cavalry.

## interfere
***verb*** to get in the way, to prevent something happening or being carried out properly.
**origin** C16, from French *s'entreferir* 'to strike', 'to collide', 'to clash'. The word was originally used about horses striking one leg against another. The current meaning dates from C18.

## intoxicate
***verb*** to be made drunk, to be made to lose control of faculties or behaviour.
**origin** ME, from Latin, *intoxicare* 'to poison', from Greek *toxikon* 'a poison for arrows'. The current meaning dates from C16.

## jazz
***noun*** type of music originating amongst Black American musicians.
**origin** C20. The word was originally used in US English, and may come from Chas, the name of a particular musician.

## jeans
***noun*** pair of casual trousers in a particular style, often made of denim.
**origin** C16, from French *jene fustian* 'fustian from Genoa'. Fustian is a type of cloth from Fostat, near Cairo in Egypt. See DENIM.

## jeep
***noun*** strong, open, four-wheeled-drive vehicle.
**origin** Second World War. The word was originally used in US English, and came from the initials GP, meaning 'general purpose' vehicle. It was influenced by 'Eugene the Jeep', a well-known, tough and resourceful cartoon character in the *Popeye* comic strip.

## jersey
***noun*** knitted sweater.
**origin** C16, name given to woollen fabric made in Jersey, Channel Islands. The current meaning dates from C19.

## jockey
***noun*** person who rides a horse in a race.
**origin** C16, diminutive of 'Jock', Scottish form of John or Jack. The word was originally used as a name for an ordinary man or lad. Later it was used to mean 'mounted messenger', or 'horse-dealer'.

## jodhpurs
***noun*** riding trousers, fitting closely below the knee and loosely above it.
**origin** C19, named after city of Jodhpur in North India, where similar trousers are worn by Indian men as everyday wear.

**jovial**
***adjective*** cheerful.
**origin** C16, from French, from Latin *jovialis* 'of Jupiter', referring to those born under the influence of the planet Jupiter.

**jubilee**
***noun*** significant anniversary, particularly 25 or 50 years.
**origin** ME, from Latin *jubilaeus annua* 'year of jubilee', from Hebrew *yobel* 'ram's horn trumpet' which was blown to mark the beginning of a jubilee year, celebrated once every 50 years.

**juggernaut**
***noun*** huge, powerful vehicle.
**origin** C19, from Hindi, from Sanskrit *Jagannatha* 'lord of the world' or 'great force'. 'Juggernaut' is the name given to the form of the god Krishna, worshipped in Puri, whose image is dragged through the streets on a huge float.

**jukebox**
***noun*** machine that automatically plays a pre-selected record when a coin is inserted.
**origin** C20. The word was originally used in US English, and comes from Gullah *juke* 'disorderly, wicked'. Cheap roadside restaurants providing music came to be known as 'jukes', hence *juke* + 'box'.

**kaleidoscope**
***noun*** cardboard tube that can be held to the eye and which contains mirrors and pieces of coloured glass that form changing patterns when rotated.
**origin** C19, from Greek *kalos* 'beautiful' + *eidos* 'form' + *scope* 'look at'.

**karate**
***noun*** oriental system of unarmed combat using the hands and feet.
**origin** from Japanese *kara* 'empty' + *te* 'hand'.

**kayak**
***noun*** type of canoe with watertight covering and small opening to sit in.
**origin** C18, from Inuit *qayaq*.

**knight**
***noun*** mounted soldier who served a particular lord or king in medieval times. The current meaning is 'someone awarded a title'.
**origin** OE *cniht* 'boy, youth or servant'. The current meaning dates from C16.

**laser**
***noun*** machine that produces narrow, parallel beams of intense light, used for cutting and drilling.
**origin** 1960s, acronym from '**l**ight **a**mplification by **s**timulated **e**mission of **r**adiation'. The first laser was built by US physicist T. H. Maiman in 1960. Laser beams have many uses, including holography, medicine, industry and telecommunications.

**loot**
***noun*** goods taken by theft.
***verb*** to steal from shops or houses left unprotected after a violent event.
**origin** C19, from Sanskrit *lunth* 'to rob'.

**luxury**
***noun*** state of great comfort and extravagant living.
**origin** C17, from French *luxurie*, *luxure*, from Latin *luxus* 'excess'.

**magazine**
***noun*** 1) periodical publication, usually covers a particular subject, contains separate articles, illustrations, advertisements; 2) the compartment in a gun for cartridges.
**origin** C16, from Arabic *makzan* 'store-house'. 'Magazine' was originally a general word for store-house, but by late C16 came to mean 'a store of ammunition'. In C18, books containing articles by different writers became known as *magazines*, literally meaning 'a store-house of information'.

**mandarin**
***noun*** small citrus fruit with loose yellow/orange skin.
**origin** late C18, from French *mandarine*, perhaps from 'Mandarin', the title of Imperial Chinese officials, who wore yellow-coloured robes.

**margarine**
***noun*** butter substitute made from vegetable oil or animal fat.
**origin** C19, from French *margarique*, from Greek *margaron* 'pearl'. Margarine was developed in France in C19, and the fat used in the manufacturing process had a pearl-like appearance.

**mascot**
***noun*** something that is meant to bring good luck or to represent a particular activity or organisation.
**origin** C19, from French *mascotte* 'little witch'.

**measles**
***noun*** infectious disease causing a rash on the skin.
**origin** C14, from Dutch *masel* 'pustule', often confused with the old word *mesel*, which meant 'leprosy'.

**migraine**
***noun*** severe headache, often affecting one side of the head, and accompanied by sickness and blurred vision.
**origin** ME, from Greek *hemi* 'half' + *kranion* 'skull'.

**naughty**
***adjective*** badly-behaved, disobedient.
**origin** ME *naught* 'nothing'. The word originally meant 'someone who had nothing'. From late ME it began to mean 'wicked'.

**newt**
***noun*** small amphibian with lungs.
**origin** ME *an ewt*. It became 'a newt' due to wrong division.

**nickname**
***noun*** familiar name given to a person or object.
**origin** ME *eke-name*, from OE *eke* 'also'. The word became divided, so 'an eke-name' became 'a neke name' which became 'a nickname'.

**nostalgia**
***noun*** sentimental longing for places or situations in the past.
**origin** C18, from Greek *nostos* 'return home' + *algos* 'pain'. The word originally meant 'homesickness'.

**ocean**
***noun*** large sea.
**origin** ME, from Greek *okeanos* 'the great river' which was thought to encircle the earth.

**ogre**
***noun*** fierce human-eating giant in folk tales.
**origin** ME, from French, first used in the fairy stories of the French writer Perrault in 1697.

**opera**
***noun*** drama set to music, where dialogue is sung not spoken.
**origin** C17, from Italian, literally 'work, labour'.

**orientate**
***verb*** to get one's bearings.
**origin** C19, from OE, literally 'to face the east', from Latin *oriri* 'to rise'. Churches are traditionally orientated, that is, built with their altars at the east end. 'Orienteering' originally came into English in 1940s from Swedish *orientering* (the sport originated in Sweden).

**ozone**
***noun*** colourless, strong-smelling toxic gas, formed from oxygen and ultraviolet light.
**origin** C19, from Greek *ozein* 'to smell', named by scientist C. F. Schonbein.

**pal** informal
***noun*** friend or mate.
**origin** C17, from Romany, based on Sanskrit *bhrātr* 'brother'.

**palaver**
***noun*** fuss; long tedious discussion.
**origin** C18, from Portuguese *palavra* 'word', from Latin *parabola* 'comparison'. The word originally meant 'a discussion between tribespeople and traders'.

**parasol**
***noun*** light umbrella used to give shade from sun.
**origin** C17, from Italian *para* 'protect against' + *sole* 'sun'. See UMBRELLA.

**piano**
***noun*** musical instrument with metal strings which are struck by hammers when keys are pressed, short for *pianoforte*.
**origin** C18, from Italian. The instrument was designed by Cristofori to play soft (*piano*) and loud (*forte*).

**planet**
***noun*** heavenly body moving around a star.
**origin** ME, from old French *planete*, from Latin *planeta*, from Greek *planetes* 'wanderer'.

**posh** informal
***adjective*** smart, expensive.
**origin** C19 slang word for a dandy, commonly used in big towns throughout England. It is often thought that 'posh' came from **p**ort **o**ut **s**tarboard **h**ome, referring to the kind of people who travelled between England and India and could afford the most comfortable accommodation on the shady side of a ship.

**primrose**
***noun*** small, pale yellow spring flower.
**origin** ME, probably from Latin *prima rose* 'first rose'.

**puny**
***adjective*** small, skinny.
**origin** C16, from French *puis ne* 'later birth'. The word originally meant a junior or younger person – a 'puisne judge' in legal language is a junior judge.

**pyjamas**
***noun*** night-wear consisting in England of trousers and a jacket.
**origin** C19, from Urdu *payejama*, from Persian *paye* 'leg' + Hindi *jama* 'clothing'. In some Asian countries, pyjamas are loose trousers with a drawstring waist, worn by men and women.

**radar**
***noun*** system used to locate or track an object at a distance, using radio waves that are reflected back from a solid surface onto a screen.
**origin** 1930, acronym of **ra**dio **d**etecting **a**nd **r**anging.

**rascal**
***noun*** mischievous, cheeky person.
**origin** ME, literally 'member of a rabble', from French *rascaille* 'rabble'.

**robot**
***noun*** machine designed to function in place of a human.
**origin** 1920s, from Czech *robota* 'forced labour', used by Karel Capek to mean 'mechanical labour' in his play *Rossum's Universal Robots*.

**rowdy**
***adjective*** noisy, disorderly.
**origin** C19. The word was originally used in US English to mean 'lawless', 'someone from the backwoods'. Origin unknown.

**safari**
***noun*** expedition to observe or hunt animals in Africa.
**origin** C19, from Kiswahili, from Arabic *safara* 'to travel'.

**saffron**
***noun*** food flavouring and dye made from the stigmas of a crocus.
**origin** ME, from Arabic *za'farān*. The town of Saffron Walden, Essex takes its name from the crocuses that were grown in the surrounding fields during the Middle Ages.

**scone**
***noun*** small soft cake of flour, usually eaten with butter.
**origin** C16, shortened version of German *schonbrot* or Dutch *schoonbroot*, meaning 'fine bread'.

**shambles**
***noun*** mess, muddle.
**origin** ME, from Latin *scamnum* 'bench or stool'. It came to mean 'butcher's table', then 'meat market', then 'slaughterhouse', then in C18 'a scene of bloodshed'.

**shampoo**
***noun*** liquid used to clean, e.g. hair, carpets.
**origin** C18, from Hindi *campo* 'press'. The word originally meant 'massage'.

**shelter**
***noun*** protection, usually from bad weather.
**origin** C16, possibly alteration of *sheltron* 'phalanx', from OE *scieldtruma* 'shield troop'. A phalanx is a collection of people or objects joined together, usually for strength.

**silk**
***noun*** soft fibre produced by silkworms in making cocoons, used to make thread and fabric.
**origin** OE *sioloc*, from Latin *sericum*, based on Greek *Seres*, the name given to the inhabitants of the Far East from where silk first came to Europe.

**sinister**
***adjective*** the impression that something unpleasant or evil is going to happen.
**origin** ME, meaning 'malicious', 'underhand', from French *sinistre*, from Latin *sinister* 'left', as in 'left-handed', 'left-side'.

**slogan**
***noun*** short memorable phrase, usually used to advertise.
**origin** C16, from Scottish Gaelic *sluagh* 'army' + *gairm* 'shout', historically a Highland war cry.

**smash**
***verb*** to break violently.
**origin** C18 imitative, probably a combination of words such as 'smite', 'smack', 'bash', 'mash', etc.

**smog**
***noun*** foggy weather conditions combined with smoke or traffic fumes.
**origin** C20, a combination of 'smoke' and 'fog'.

**snack**
***noun*** small amount of food, usually eaten between meals.
**origin** ME, from Dutch *snac(k)* 'snap', 'bite'. The current meaning dates from C17.

**stupid**
***adjective*** lacking in intelligence.
**origin** C16, from Latin *stupere* 'be amazed or stunned'. 'Stupendous', meaning 'amazing' or 'stunning' is closer to the original meaning.

**tabloid**
***noun*** newspaper with small sheets, half the size of a broadsheet.
**origin** late C19, originally the name for a medicine sold in tablet form. It became the term used for any medicinal tablet. The current use is figurative, suggesting 'small, easy to take'.

## taboo
***adjective*** social or religious reasons for prohibiting a particular practice.
**origin** C18, from Tongan *tabu* 'set apart', 'forbidden', introduced into English by Captain Cook.

## talent
***noun*** natural skill or ability
**origin** OE *talente*, from Latin *talenta* 'weight', 'sum of money'. The sense in which talent is used today is figurative – someone who is talented is someone who is weighted, or favoured, in a particular direction.

## tank
***noun*** 1) large receptacle or container for liquid or gas, usually made of metal;
2) armoured vehicle that moves on articulated tracks.
**origin** C17, perhaps from Gujarati *tānkũ* or Marathi *tānkẽ* 'underground cistern', from Sanskrit *tadāga* 'pond'. The word 'tank' was used as a code-name for the armoured vehicle when it was first manufactured in 1915.

## tawdry
***adjective*** cheap, garish.
**origin** C17, short for *tawdry lace* (short for *St Audrey's lace*), silk lace or ribbon worn around the neck in C16 and C17. St Audrey was the patron saint of Ely, where tawdry lace was traditionally sold at a fair.

## thug
***noun*** violent person.
**origin** C17, from Hindi *thag* 'swindler, thief'. A Thug was a member of a murderous religious sect who followed the goddess Kali and killed their victims in a ritual manner.

## toboggan
***noun*** long, flat vehicle on runners used for travelling over ice or snow.
**origin** C19, from Canadian French *tabaganne*, from Micmac *topaĝan* 'sled'. Micmac is the language of the Mi'kmaq Native American people inhabiting the Maritime Provinces in Canada; now only approx. 8,000 speakers.

## tulip
***noun*** brightly coloured spring bulb with cup-shaped flowers.
**origin** late C16, from Persian *dulband* 'turban', because of the shape of the flower.

## tycoon
***noun*** wealthy, powerful person in business or industry.
**origin** C19, from Japanese *taikun* 'great lord' or 'prince'. The title 'tycoon' was wrongly used by foreigners in Japan to refer to the shogun, who was a hereditary Japanese military commander-in-chief. The word was first used in America to describe powerful politicians or businessmen, and also used during the American Civil War to refer to Abraham Lincoln.

## umbrella
***noun*** circular shade made from material stretched over a frame as protection from rain.
**origin** C17, from Italian *ombrella* 'little shade', from Latin *umbra* 'shade'. See PARASOL.

## urchin
***noun*** naughty child, usually raggedly dressed.
**origin** ME *urchon* 'hedgehog'. The word also meant 'goblin'.

## vandal
***noun*** someone who deliberately destroys or violates property.
**origin** C17, from Latin *vandalus*. In C4 and C5 a tribe of Germanic people called the Vandals invaded Western Europe and North Africa, destroying many cities.

**vanguard**
***noun*** group of people leading the way in new developments or ideas.
**origin** ME, literally 'the front ranks of an army', from French *avangarde* (see Appendix 1), from *avant* 'before' + *garde* 'guard'.

**velvet**
***noun*** material, usually cotton, with short soft pile on one side.
**origin** ME, from French *velu* 'velvety', from Latin *villus* 'tuft', 'down'.

**victim**
***noun*** person who is harmed as a result of circumstances or someone else's actions.
**origin** C15, from Latin *victima* 'an animal killed for a religious sacrifice'.

**villain**
***noun*** criminal or wicked person.
**origin** ME *villein* 'a simple person', 'a villager'. A villein was someone who, under feudal law, paid dues to a landowner.

**wimp** informal
***noun*** weak and cowardly person.
**origin** 1920s. Origin uncertain, perhaps from 'whimper'.

**window**
***noun*** opening in a building or vehicle usually filled with glass or similar to allow light to come in.
**origin** ME, from Old Norse *vindauga*, from *vindr* 'wind' + *auga* 'eye'.

**yob** informal
***noun*** rude, noisy and aggressive boy or young man.
**origin** C19, back slang for 'boy'.

**zany**
***adjective*** unconventionally amusing.
**origin** C16, from Italian *zani*, the Venetian version of the name *Gianni* or *Giovanni*. During C16–C18, a popular entertainment was the *commedia dell'arte*, improvised comedy based on stock characters. *Zani* was the name of the servant or clown.

**zip**
***noun*** type of fastener, with metal or plastic hooks that lock together when a slide is pulled over them.
**origin** C19, imitative.

## Loan words

Some words and phrases have been adopted by English speakers and have become part of the language. They have not been modified because they mean just what they say, and often become clumsy when translated. They are known as loan words.

**ad hoc**
not planned in advance
Latin *for this*

**ad infinitum** [in-fin-**eye**-tum]
without limit, for ever
Latin *to infinity*

**à la carte**
separate items on a menu
French *from the menu*

**alfresco**
in the open air
Italian *in the fresh air*

**au fait** [oh-**fay**]
being familiar with something, knowing how to do something well
French *to the point*

**au gratin** [oh-**grat**-an]
cooked with a topping of breadcrumbs and/or cheese
French

**au revoir** [oh-rev-**wahr**]
goodbye
French *until (I, we) see (you) again*

**avant-garde** [av-ahn-**gard**]
innovative style, usually in art or literature
French *vanguard*

**bona fide** [bo-ner-**fy**-de]
genuine
Latin *in good faith*

**bon voyage** [bon-vwah-**azj**]
have a good journey
French *good journey*

**c'est la vie** [say-la-**vee**]
that's life
French

**compos mentis**
in your right mind, sane
Latin *having control of the mind*

**cordon bleu** [kor-don-**blur**]
very good (of chefs, cooks, cooking)
French *blue ribbon*

**corps de ballet** [cor-der-**bal**-ay]
the 'chorus' of dancers in a ballet company
French

**crème de la crème** [**krem**-der-la-**krem**]
the very best
French *cream of the cream*

**curriculum vitae** [curriculum-**veet**-eye]
an account of a person's education, qualifications and career to date
Latin *course of life*

**déjà vu** [day-ja-**voo**]
a feeling that you have already experienced what is happening
French *already seen*

**en masse** [on-**mass**]
altogether
French *in a mass*

**en route** [on-**root**]
on the way
French

**eureka** [yoor-**eek**-a]
I've found it!
Greek

**faux pas** [foh-**pah**]
mistake, usually doing or saying something out of place
French *false step*

**hoi polloi**
the ordinary people
Greek *the many*

**Homo sapiens**
human beings as a species
Latin *wise man*

**hors-d'oeuvre** [or-**derv**]
first course of a meal, starter
French *outside work*

**in memoriam**
in remembrance
Latin

**in situ** [in-**sit**-yoo]
in its original place
Latin

**joie de vivre** [zjwah-de-**veevr**]
a feeling of enjoying life
French *joy of life*

**laissez-faire** [lay-say-**fair**]
leaving be (often referring to an official policy of not interfering)
French *let (them) act*

**modus operandi** [moh-dus-op-er-**and**-eye]
way of working [sometimes abbreviated to MO]
Latin

**nom de plume**
pen-name
French [but not used in France]

**non sequitur** [non-**sek**-wit-er]
not following logically on
Latin *it does not follow*

**nota bene** [noh-ta-**bay**-nay]
note well, usually shortened to NB
Latin *note well*

**objet d'art** [ob-zjay-**dar**]
a small piece of art or design
French *object of art*

**par excellence** [par-eks-el-**ahns**]
better, more than, all the rest
French *by excellence*

**pas de deux** [pah-der-**der**]
a dance for two people
French *step of two*

**per annum**
yearly
Latin

**per capita**
for each person
Latin for *heads*

**pièce de résistance** [**pee**-ess-de-ray-**zees**-tahns]
the item that is so important it is kept until last
French

**placebo** [plas-**ee**-boh]
something harmless given as if it were medicine in order to reassure patient
Latin *I shall be pleasing*

**poste restante** [post-rest-**ahnt**]
a service at a main post office, where mail is kept for individuals to collect
French *letters remaining*

**quid pro quo** [kwid-pro-kwoh]
something given or done in return for something given or done
Latin *something for something*

**raison d'etre** [ray-zon-**detr**]
a reason for existence
French *reason for being*

**rigor mortis**
stiffening of the body after death
Latin *stiffness of death*

**RIP (requiescat in pace)**
may (he, she) rest in peace
Latin

**sang-froid** [sahng-**fwah**]
calmness in dangerous or difficult circumstances
French *cold blood*

**savoir-faire** [sav-wahr-**fair**]
a knowledge of social behaviour
French *to know to do*

**sotto voce** [sot-oh-**voh**-chay]
in a very quiet voice
Italian *under the voice*

**status quo**
the state of things as they are, or before change
Latin *the state in which*

**terra firma**
dry land
Latin *firm land*

**tete-à-tete** [tet-ah-tet]
private conversation
French *head to head*

**vis-à-vis** [veez-a-**vee**]
in relation to
French *face to face*

# Appendix 2

## Prefixes

Prefixes are added to words to alter or qualify the meaning. They mostly derive from Greek and Latin. Prefixes are not usually words in their own right, but they do have meaning, and provide clues about the whole word. The following is a list of some the most commonly occurring prefixes.

**amb-** on both sides

**ante-** before, in time or position

**anti-** opposed to or against

**bi-** two

**co-** together, jointly

**counter-** against

**de-** away from, reversal of

**di-** double

**dis-** the opposite of

**ex-** out, outside

**extra-** outside, beyond

**fore-** before

**homo-** same, like

**im-** in, not

**inter-** between, among

**intra-** on the inside

**mal-** evil, ill

**manu-** hand

**milli-** one thousandth part of

**mis-** a lack of, wrong

**neo-** new, recent

**omni-** all

**per-** through

**post-** after

**pre-** before

**quadr-** four

**re-** again

**retro-** backwards

**semi-** half

**sub-** under, beneath

**super-** over, above

**trans-** across

**un-** not

**with-** against, back

# Bibliography & Acknowledgements

## Bibliography

*The New Oxford Dictionary of English*, OUP, 1998

Beal G., *Kingfisher Book of Words*, *Kingfisher Books*, 1991

Bryson B., *Mother Tongue*, Penguin Books, 1990

Crystal D., *The Cambridge Encyclopedia of Language*, CUP, 1987

Whitcut J., *The Penguin Book of Exotic Words*, Penguin Books, 1996

## Acknowledgements

*The New Oxford Dictionary of English*, OUP, 1998

Crystal D., *The Cambridge Encyclopedia of Language*, CUP 1987